SKILLED AND VOCATIONAL TRADES

BECOME A
REAL ESTATE APPRAISER

by Tammy Gagne

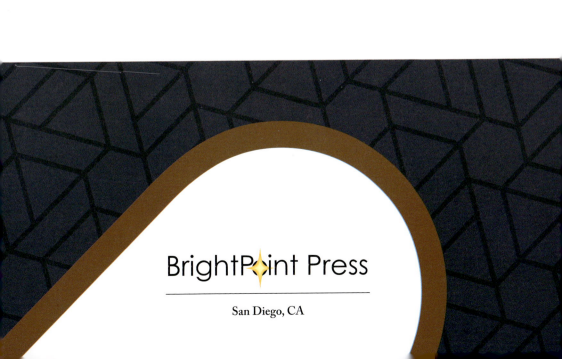

BrightPoint Press

San Diego, CA

© 2024 BrightPoint Press
an imprint of ReferencePoint Press, Inc.
Printed in the United States

For more information, contact:
BrightPoint Press
PO Box 27779
San Diego, CA 92198
www.BrightPointPress.com

ALL RIGHTS RESERVED.

No part of this work covered by the copyright hereon may be reproduced or used in any form or by any means—graphic, electronic, or mechanical, including photocopying, recording, taping, web distribution, or information storage retrieval systems—without the written permission of the publisher.

LIBRARY OF CONGRESS CATALOGING-IN-PUBLICATION DATA

Names: Gagne, Tammy, author.
Title: Become a real estate appraiser / by Tammy Gagne.
Description: San Diego, CA: BrightPoint Press, [2024] | Series: Skilled and vocational trades | Includes bibliographical references and index. | Audience: Ages 13 | Audience: Grades 7-9
Identifiers: LCCN 2023009764 (print) | LCCN 2023009765 (eBook) | ISBN 9781678206901 (hardcover) | ISBN 9781678206918 (eBook)
Subjects: LCSH: Real property--Valuation--Juvenile literature. | Real estate appraisers--Juvenile literature.
Classification: LCC HD1387 .G336 2024 (print) | LCC HD1387 (eBook) | DDC 333.33/2--dc23/eng/20230418
LC record available at https://lccn.loc.gov/2023009764
LC ebook record available at https://lccn.loc.gov/2023009765

CONTENTS

AT A GLANCE	4
INTRODUCTION	6
WHY BECOME A REAL ESTATE APPRAISER?	
CHAPTER ONE	12
WHAT DOES A REAL ESTATE APPRAISER DO?	
CHAPTER TWO	28
WHAT TRAINING DO REAL ESTATE APPRAISERS NEED?	
CHAPTER THREE	42
WHAT IS LIFE LIKE AS A REAL ESTATE APPRAISER?	
CHAPTER FOUR	58
WHAT IS THE FUTURE FOR REAL ESTATE APPRAISERS?	
Glossary	74
Source Notes	75
For Further Research	76
Index	78
Image Credits	79
About the Author	80

AT A GLANCE

- Real estate appraisers are hired by homeowners or lenders to check the value of a home or other type of property.

- The value of a property can change based on the economy, the surrounding neighborhoods, and the property's size and condition.

- Appraisers can specialize in different types of real estate, including condominiums, commercial property, and even farms.

- Before trainees become appraisers, they need to take appraiser-related courses. They also need to pass an exam and work with a certified appraiser. This can take anywhere from a few months to a few years.

- Doing math such as algebra and geometry can be important for real estate appraisers when they calculate the value of a property.

- An appraiser must be detailed oriented, keeping schedules organized and checking emails daily.

- Real estate appraisers get paid according to how many projects they complete. Their pay differs depending on the state the appraiser lives in.

- People are working to make the real estate appraiser industry more diverse.

INTRODUCTION

WHY BECOME A REAL ESTATE APPRAISER?

Sierra Alden enjoys challenging herself. She had worked in both banking and insurance before. But she became bored when there was no more for her to learn. She decided to look for a new career. She wanted new challenges every day. She became a real estate appraiser trainee.

Real estate property includes apartments.

Real estate is property that includes land, buildings, or both. Appraisers decide what a property's value is. This information helps the seller set a price.

Each day in this field is a bit different. Alden told *Working RE* magazine, "I really

Appraisers can do walk-through appraisals with homeowners.

enjoy learning and problem-solving—and there's so much of that in appraising. Every time I walk into a house or do a report, there's always a problem I need to solve."[1] For example, a seller may set a high price for a home. But this may not be accurate.

The seller may need to fix parts of the property to make it worth the high price.

Alden also enjoys the variety of duties in appraising. Her day might begin by inspecting a property with her **supervisor**. An inspection can mean meeting new homeowners. Another part of the job is writing reports. These reports have a detailed explanation of a property's value. Alden can work on her reports at the office or at home. She can even finish her work late in the evening if she wants. Alden can often set her own schedule around other parts of her life.

The value of real estate can change quickly. Prices rise when more people want to buy property. This is called rising demand. When demand goes down, prices drop. This makes appraising a constantly changing field. Technology is also changing real estate. Software can now create sketches of properties. These drawings show the property's layout and measurements. Appraisers used to create these drawings by hand.

Some people worry that technology might take over some appraisal work. It could even replace appraisers one day.

Appraisers can use technology to make drawings of properties and floor plans. Then they can add their own notes and calculations by hand.

But Alden isn't worried. She explains, "I think appraisers that are willing to adapt, embrace new technologies, and continue learning will be around for a long time. That's why I made the decision to become an appraiser."[2]

CHAPTER ONE

WHAT DOES A REAL ESTATE APPRAISER DO?

Real estate appraisers are important for when people buy homes. People who buy their house with cash do not need an appraisal. However, people who want to get a mortgage must get an appraisal. A mortgage is a type of loan. Many people interested in buying property need

Appraisers are an important part of the process of buying a home.

to borrow money from lenders such as banks. Lenders take risks when they give mortgages. They can't be sure whether

Working with an appraiser can be the first step in bringing a homeowner's renovation ideas to life.

people will give the money back. Hiring an

appraiser can lower that risk. Appraisers

can show lenders that the property is worth

the price. They can also protect borrowers from paying too much. Buyers usually pay for the appraisal. However, lenders choose the appraiser. This is to make sure that everything is done fairly.

Appraisals are not just needed when people are buying homes. Homeowners might want an appraisal too. They need an appraisal if they want to get a loan for renovating their house. Real estate agents can also hire appraisers. Appraisers can help agents figure out the price of the home before it goes on the market. They can also show agents any concerns they might have

Appraisers need to inspect property carefully.

with the property. This helps agents and sellers adjust the price accordingly.

APPRAISAL WORK

An appraisal usually begins with an on-site visit. Houses are called residential property. To appraise houses, appraisers look at the home's interior and exterior. They walk around and take photos. They make notes about the building's size and condition. Appraisals can take about 20 to 30 minutes. The time varies based on the size of the property.

    The appraiser must make sure the property meets all health and safety codes. A common safety code says that chimneys must be properly taken care of. This is so that dangerous gases cannot build up inside the house. More careful examinations are done by a home inspector.

The inspector looks for defects in the house. An appraiser only looks for the value in the home.

Appraisers will also look for upgrades. Many homeowners make improvements in their homes. These changes can increase the home's value. Upgrades can include adding a deck or a swimming pool. A finished basement is another common upgrade.

Bob Musinski is a finance writer. He explains that the cost of nearby homes also affects an appraisal. He says, "The most relevant [nearby homes] have many

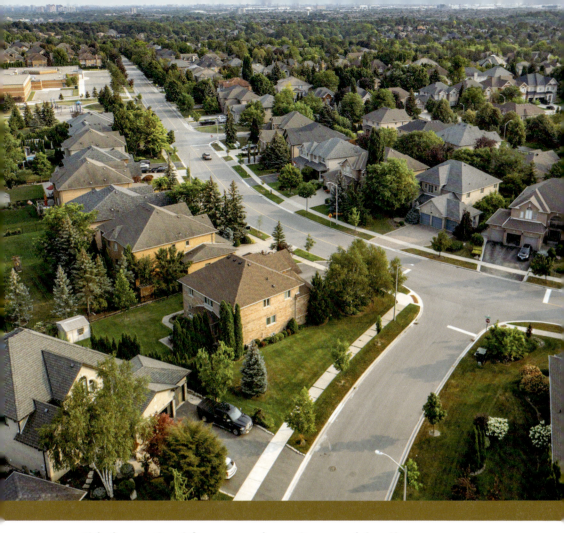

It is important for appraisers to consider the property's neighborhood.

of the same characteristics as the home in question."[3] A house will usually have a similar value to the houses surrounding it. People can find the cost of properties in

Appraisers can specialize in appraising commercial properties.

government records. Appraisers can also find this information in the Multiple Listing Service (MLS). Real estate professionals record sale information in this database.

Appraisers combine the information they gathered from their on-site visit and their research. Research can take around 48 to 72 hours. This is all used to make a detailed report. The report lists an official estimate of the property's value. This whole process usually takes 3 to 7 days.

TYPES OF REAL ESTATE APPRAISERS

There are several types of real estate appraisers. Some only work with regular residential property. This includes single-family houses or single **condominium** units. Others may work with entire multi-unit dwellings.

Examples of these include duplexes and apartment buildings.

Appraisers can work with commercial or industrial property. Commercial property may include a restaurant or a store. It can be any business that offers goods or services. Industrial properties are usually used to manufacture goods. Appraising these properties is often harder. It usually takes longer than appraising homes. This is partly because they have a wide variety of sizes, shapes, and purposes.

Some appraisers specialize in other types of real estate, such as farms. Other appraisers find property values for court cases. For example, couples may fight about what should happen to a property in a divorce. Lawyers often hire appraisers when this happens. There are even appraisers who review the work of other

FARMLAND APPRAISAL

When appraising a farm, appraisers look at several things before figuring out the cost. They look at the size and layout of the property. Appraisers check if the farmland is easy to access. They also look at the type of land the farm is on. For example, buyers might not want the farmland if it has a lot of rocks and hills. Land with good soil and flat land has a higher value. Also, the land might have more value if people can easily access water.

Appraisers usually don't get paid the same amount every month.

appraisers. They do this to make sure the

appraisals are correct.

WHAT REAL ESTATE APPRAISERS EARN

Real estate appraisers usually work by assignment. This means that their employers give them one project at a time. For this reason, appraisers' pay is often based on the number of appraisals they do. Their pay can be unpredictable. But appraisers can make a lot of money if they have many assignments.

Terrence Bilodeau made only $17,000 the year he became a real estate appraiser trainee in Texas. Bilodeau wanted to earn more. After getting licensed, he opened his own appraising business. Each US state has its own licensing program. Programs make sure that appraisers have the necessary skills. Bilodeau made more than $80,000 his first year in business. He was able to adjust his schedule however he wanted. He also charged his clients higher fees. After opening his business, Bilodeau got more appraisal requests.

Appraisers can work for themselves. They can also work for companies. Larger companies have more employees. They can take on more work than smaller businesses. As appraisers gain experience, they can earn more money. They can also move into management roles. This means they oversee the work of other appraisers.

WHERE TO SPECIALIZE

Most appraisers begin in residential work. They may later move to commercial work. An appraiser needs another license to work on commercial appraisals. Each type of license involves education, training, and testing. A certified general appraiser is the highest level. Most of these appraisers work with large commercial developers. These are businesses that buy property to construct office buildings, shopping malls, and other spaces. Some people know right away what kind of appraising they want to do. Others may not decide until they have worked in the field a while.

CHAPTER TWO

WHAT TRAINING DO REAL ESTATE APPRAISERS NEED?

Becoming a real estate appraiser requires time and preparation. The exact steps depend on the state. The steps might look different based on the type of appraiser a person wants to become. Advanced types of appraising need more

People who want to be real estate appraisers need to complete specific training and education.

education and training. Some states allow

people to begin training even if they didn't

get a college degree. But they will likely need a degree before becoming licensed or certified.

Phillip Ethington runs an appraisal company in Austin, Texas. Ethington explained, "Licensed appraisers often are not required to have a four-year degree

USEFUL EDUCATION

Degrees related to math or business are helpful for someone interested in real estate appraisal. A bachelor's degree in any field of study fulfills most appraisal requirements. But people who have studied accounting or business may find it easier to learn the tasks involved in appraising. Students can even earn degrees in real estate itself.

as long as they satisfy other education requirements."[4] For example, people can get an associate's degree in a related field. They may qualify to become an appraiser by earning a certain number of college credits.

Appraisers in the field also need to keep learning. Licenses and other certifications expire. Most are good for between 1 and 4 years. Additional classes and tests are often needed to renew certifications. Real estate laws and values can change over time. Knowing the latest information is important in this job.

Trainees need to pass their appraisal exams before they become official appraisers.

TRAINEE PROGRAMS

Even someone with a degree in real estate must learn how to appraise property.

For this reason, finding a position as a trainee is the next step. A trainee must take the real estate appraisal courses the state requires. For example, in Washington, there are three courses required. It takes about 75 hours to complete the courses. Students must pass a 3-hour exam at the end of each course. The courses are available online in every US state. Some states might require more coursework.

Trainees also need hands-on experience. They must work with a certified appraiser for a total of 15 hours. Some states also require trainees to do a certain number of inspections with a supervisor. Supervisors can give trainees important advice about the job. This information can be helpful for passing the trainee exam.

After finishing the 15 hours of appraisal practice, trainees take the trainee exam. Each state has its own version of the exam. Exams have questions about the state's laws about real estate appraisals. After passing this test, trainees can officially start working under supervision.

Certification requires about 1,000 hours of supervised work. For most people, this takes between 6 months and 2 years.

Trainees need to work with a skilled appraiser.

This is enough time to learn everything they must know to pass their test.

Some appraisers are not interested in training others. They may worry that trainees will become their competition. Appraisers who are willing to take on trainees usually keep them as employees. Companies can make more money if they have more appraisers to share the workload.

THE DIFFERENCE BETWEEN LICENSING AND CERTIFICATION

The biggest difference between licensed and certified appraisers is the **complexity** and value of the properties they can appraise. For example, both licensed and certified residential appraisers can work with multifamily houses with up to four units. But a licensed appraiser cannot appraise a four-unit building that is more than $1 million. A certified appraiser has no such limitations.

It can also be better for trainees to stay with the trainer for a while. This is especially true if the trainer is very skilled. Trainees are also more likely to keep working for a trainer who treats them well. Appraiser Mike Lay stated, "It seems to me that 'bosses' tend to lose trainees as soon as they get licensed, but **'mentors'** tend to keep them."[5]

Being a trainee does not pay as well as being a certified real estate appraiser. But trainees still get a paycheck. Trainees can contribute valuable work to the appraisal process. Their help can save certified appraisers time and money.

GETTING LICENSED

When trainees feel ready, they can register to take their Licensed Residential Exam. They should make sure they have finished all the requirements. These include real estate appraiser classes. They can also include any educational requirements for the level of the exam. Checking the state's website may be helpful during this step.

Even trainees who are confident in their knowledge should prepare for their test. People who study for the exam

Studying hard can help trainees do well in their licensing exam.

have the best chance of passing it. Many people do not pass the test the first time they take it. In 2021, only 61 percent of first-time test takers passed the Licensed Residential Exam.

Many online courses have practice exams. These can be especially helpful for studying. A score of 70 percent or higher is needed to pass the Licensed Residential Exam. Trainees scoring at least 80 percent on their practice exams are usually ready to take the test.

The Licensed Residential Test demonstrates that appraisers are ready for real-world work.

CHAPTER THREE

WHAT IS LIFE LIKE AS A REAL ESTATE APPRAISER?

Every real estate appraiser must learn the tasks involved in the job. Some people think these duties are easy. Others find them harder. The best real estate appraisers have good math skills. Much of this job involves working with numbers.

Learning how to measure and calculate are important skills in appraising.

An appraiser might take measurements.

They sometimes convert measurements

into other units. Appraisers need to understand and use decimals, fractions, and percentages. Appraisers must also calculate the value of each part of the property. This may include an updated kitchen or bathroom. Doing all of this math takes both time and effort.

WHERE REAL ESTATE APPRAISERS WORK

Real estate appraisers work in different industries. Many work for local or state governments. Some work for real estate firms. Others work for financial institutions. Still others are self-employed. People who enjoy having more independence and control choose this option.

Tim Lane is an appraiser. He says that he uses algebra and geometry regularly. He admits that he didn't enjoy math in school. In fact, he says he wasn't comfortable with all the math he had to do as an appraiser at first. But once Lane figured out how he could apply his knowledge in his job, doing math became a lot easier.

OTHER IMPORTANT SKILLS

A real estate appraiser needs to juggle a variety of duties. Staying organized while having a busy schedule is important. Appraisers who are flexible will have an easier time. They must often work

Having an organized schedule is important for appraisers.

many hours. They need to work around

other people's schedules. Sometimes

buyers need an appraisal as soon as possible. Other times, buyers may need to reschedule an appointment. Being patient is also a plus. Appraisers want to do their work quickly. But they need to take enough time to find an accurate value for each property.

Good communication skills are also important. Appraisers deal with different types of people. They talk to real estate agents, bankers, and home buyers. They must sometimes explain their work to buyers. Good appraisers understand that customer service is part of the job. They must be polite and show up on time for appointments. They must meet deadlines.

Dealing with difficult people is also part of being a real estate appraiser. Sometimes an appraisal comes in lower than the planned sale price of a property. This can cause a bank to deny a loan. A homeowner or buyer might get angry when this happens. Maureen Sweeney is an appraiser. She wrote an article about this part of the job. Sweeney pointed out that banks can turn down buyers for loans for many reasons. But she added, "Because the appraiser

THE PROS AND CONS OF BEING A REAL ESTATE APPRAISER

PROS	CONS
There are many well-paying jobs available in this industry.	It can take a while to reach the highest salaries in this profession.
Real estate appraisers can create their own work schedules much of the time.	It may be difficult to find an appraiser willing to take on a trainee.
Appraisers are always meeting new people and performing a variety of tasks.	The pay may vary depending on the number of assignments one receives.

Before becoming a real estate appraiser, people need to carefully look at the negatives and positives of the job.

is typically the only party in the mortgage process who meets the homeowner in person, the appraiser may become the sole target of the homeowner's disappointment,

SKILLS VERSUS REQUIREMENTS

All real estate appraisers must have the same basic skills. But the exact requirements for this job vary. For example, states often require different levels of education or testing. The type of appraising also matters. A person may need only an associate's degree to become a residential appraiser. But a bachelor's degree might be necessary for commercial appraisers. Some states require appraisers to be licensed while others do not.

even if the reason for rejection of a loan has nothing to do with the **market value** of the property."[6]

Appraisers must stay **unbiased** when doing their work. Laws stop appraisers from basing any part of their appraisal on a person's gender, sex, or sexual orientation. Appraisers also cannot base their appraisal on a person's race, age, or mental or physical impairment. Those who have bias of any kind toward a client must withdraw from the assignment. If they don't, they can be fined, lose their appraisal license, or even go to jail.

AN APPRAISER'S TYPICAL DAY

Many real estate appraisers start their days by checking their phone. They might need to look at their email messages. Their schedule is always changing. Sometimes assignments get added at the last minute. Other appointments may get cancelled or rescheduled. Knowing what is on the agenda is the best way to stay on top of the work.

Chris Dolland is a real estate appraiser in Texas. He usually plans his appraisals for the morning. This helps him avoid being outdoors during the hotter afternoon

Checking emails and appointments is important at the beginning and end of an appraiser's day.

During a busy week, an appraiser may perform more than ten appraisals per week.

weather. He performs between one and

three appraisals each day. Many appraisers

work evenings and weekends. But odd hours like these are rare for Dolland.

Dolland usually heads to his office after his last appraisal. He spends the afternoon writing his reports. He likes doing them when all the information is fresh in his mind. He starts his property sketches on site. He often finishes the drawings there too. Other times, he puts finishing touches on them at the office. He refers to his notes for this step.

Some clients like having their inspection done later in the day. When this is the case, Dolland heads straight to the office in the morning. He knows that being flexible is part of the job. A morning at the office usually means writing reports from the previous day's inspections. His reports are typically due within a day or so. This makes report writing a daily task on his calendar.

Sometimes Dolland needs to do **revisions** on a report. Most are simple changes. Some are requests for additional information. He does this type of work after he finishes his fresh reports for the day. Dolland likes that his work is both varied and predictable.

Writing an appraisal report is one of the last steps in a home sale.

CHAPTER FOUR

WHAT IS THE FUTURE FOR REAL ESTATE APPRAISERS?

The demand for real estate appraisers is strongly linked to the economy. When the number of real estate sales increases, the demand for appraisers rises. Demand falls when fewer properties are being bought and sold. Growing populations and

There is a bigger need for appraisers when more homes are being sold.

expanding businesses affect the real estate market. As families grow, they need larger homes. Likewise, growing companies need places for their employees to work.

The US Bureau of Labor Statistics predicts that the US job market will grow

> **WHERE TO EARN THE MOST MONEY**
>
> The amount of money real estate appraisers make varies widely from one area to another. In 2021, the best paid appraisers worked in Washington, DC. Even the lowest paid appraisers in the nation's capital made more than $60,000 that year. The average pay was more than $96,000 per year. Appraisers in Nevada, California, and Alaska also topped the list of appraisers who made the most money in the field.

about 4 percent between 2021 and 2031. For appraisers, the bureau predicts growth of about the same amount during this period. The actual growth may be a bit higher or lower. But this data shows that the future of appraisal looks promising.

Demand for appraisers may even be higher than expected in the future. One of the reasons is how many current appraisers will be retiring. In 2021, nearly half of real estate appraisers in the United States were between the ages of fifty-one and sixty-five. By 2031, many of these people will be retired. New appraisers will be needed.

A SHORTAGE OF NEW AND DIVERSE APPRAISERS

Another factor in the future of this industry is the number of people entering the field. Only a small number of people are training to replace older appraisers. In 2019, just 7 percent of appraisers had been working in the field for under 2 years. More young appraisers are needed in the field.

Jacob Williamson is a senior vice president at the Federal National Mortgage Association (Fannie Mae). In an article on the company's website, Williamson wrote, "You probably didn't hear from an appraiser

Young appraisers are needed in the industry.

on career day at school—I know I didn't.

There seems to be limited awareness of

Companies such as Fannie Mae seek to make the appraisal industry more diverse by offering scholarships to women and people of color.

the career opportunities available in the residential appraisal field."[7]

Appraisal is also one of the least diverse industries in the United States. Williamson shared that three-quarters of real estate appraisers are men. There are relatively few people of color. In 2019, just 11 percent of appraisers were racial minorities. Some experts think that increasing diversity could help lower the number of biased appraisals.

Alec Marcus was a twenty-eight-year-old appraiser in 2021. He hoped that other young people would fill the positions left empty by retirees. In an article for the MReport website, he wrote, "There is no greater time for young people to enter the real estate appraisal field than right now. What many may not realize is that an appraisal career can provide them with the level of flexibility and earning potential that they've been looking for."[8]

TECHNOLOGY IN APPRAISING

Advancing technology has made appraising quicker and easier in recent years. At one time all appraisals needed to be in person. But a lot of the data that appraisers need can be found online. Laser measuring devices and scanning software can create 3D images of properties. These tools save both time and effort.

Computer programs can make 3D renderings of properties.

Even with more technology in the field, appraisers need to do many in-person tasks.

Appraisers need to use computers to write their reports. But they do not always need to write their reports in an office. They can also write their reports outside of business hours.

Technology makes it possible for appraisers to work remotely at any time. Appraisers can do meetings through a video call. Video calls or online chats can help appraisers connect with coworkers. Many appraisers like a mixture of in-person and at-home work. But some appraisers work fully remotely. Working from home can be especially helpful for real estate appraisers starting their own businesses. It can make renting expensive office space unnecessary.

Some people worry that technology will take jobs away from appraisers in the future. Stan Humphries analyzes data for

> **MOVING UP**
>
> The best way to move up the real estate appraising ladder is for people to expand their skills. For example, a licensed residential appraiser can take the test to become a certified residential appraiser. A certified commercial appraiser can become a certified general appraiser. Being able to appraise more types of properties can be useful to employers and clients.

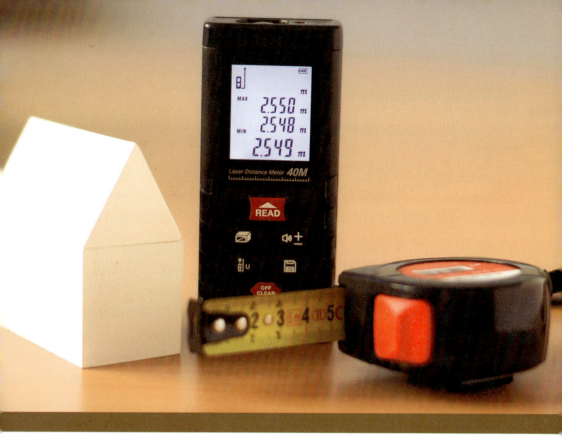

Many appraisers use technology, such as laser measuring devices, to make their job easier.

the website Zillow. He thinks it's only a matter of time until computers can do much of the work that people now do. But he doesn't think people will be removed from appraising entirely. Humans may not need to do all the math themselves. But they may still need to gather, check, and present the information that computers provide.

Real estate appraising can be an ideal job for people who enjoy doing something a little different each day. This is also a career for people who enjoy staying busy. The job is great for meeting new people regularly. This can be rewarding. In the coming years, real estate appraising job openings will only grow.

People interested in real estate can consider being a real estate appraiser.

GLOSSARY

complexity

the state of having numerous or complicated qualities

condominium

a building containing a number of individually owned dwellings

market value

the amount that a property can be sold for currently

mentors

people who help others by serving as role models

revisions

changes made to a document

supervisor

a person who oversees the work of another

unbiased

fair and impartial

SOURCE NOTES

INTRODUCTION: WHY BECOME A REAL ESTATE APPRAISER?

1. Quoted in Isaac Peck, "Profiling an Up-and-Coming (New) Appraiser," *Working RE*, n.d. www.workingre.com.

2. Quoted in Peck, "Profiling an Up-and-Coming (New) Appraiser."

CHAPTER ONE: WHAT DOES A REAL ESTATE APPRAISER DO?

3. Bob Musinski, "How Home Appraisals Work," *Forbes*, September 3, 2020. www.forbes.com.

CHAPTER TWO: WHAT TRAINING DO REAL ESTATE APPRAISERS NEED?

4. Quoted in Josephine Nesbit, "How to Become a Real Estate Appraiser," *US News and World Report*, February 28, 2022. https://realestate.usnews.com.

5. Mike Lay, "Tips for Training New Appraisers," *Working RE*, n.d. www.workingre.com.

CHAPTER THREE: WHAT IS LIFE LIKE AS A REAL ESTATE APPRAISER?

6. Maureen Sweeney, "Racial Bias in Real Estate: Is It the Appraiser's Fault?" *Working RE*, n.d. www.workingre.com.

CHAPTER FOUR: WHAT IS THE FUTURE FOR REAL ESTATE APPRAISERS?

7. Jacob Williamson, "The Intriguing Future of Appraisal Careers," *Fannie Mae*, June 3, 2019. www.fanniemae.com.

8. Alec Marcus, "What Appraisal Careers Offer Millennials/Gen Z," *MReport*, August 9, 2021. https://themreport.com.

FOR FURTHER RESEARCH

BOOKS

Rob Colson, *Jobs in Math*. New York: PowerKids Press, 2022.

Janie Havemeyer, *Carpenters on the Job*. Parker, CO: The Child's World, 2020.

Elizabeth Hobbs Voss, *Become a Construction and Building Inspector*. San Diego, CA: BrightPoint Press, 2024.

INTERNET SOURCES

"Everything You Should Know About a Home Appraisal," *Chase*, n.d. www.chase.com.

Hanna Kielar, "What Is a Home Appraisal, and How Much Does It Cost?" *Rocket Mortgage*, March 23, 2023. www.rocketmortgage.com.

Jacob Williamson, "The Intriguing Future of Appraisal Careers," *Fannie Mae*, June 3, 2019. www.fanniemae.com.

WEBSITES

The Appraisal Foundation
www.appraisalfoundation.org

The Appraisal Foundation is a national organization that sets standards for the real estate appraisal industry.

Appraisal Institute
www.appraisalinstitute.org

The Appraisal Institute is an international organization for real estate appraisers. It provides education and community for appraisers.

US Bureau of Labor Statistics
www.bls.gov

The US Bureau of Labor Statistics offers quick facts about pay, educational requirements, and more for real estate appraisers.

Alden, Sierra, 6–9, 11

Bilodeau, Terrence, 25–26
buyers, 15, 23, 47–48

certifications, 31, 34, 36

Dolland, Chris, 52, 55–56

earning money, 25–26, 60
education, 27, 29, 30, 31, 38, 50
Ethington, Phillip, 30

farms, 22, 23

Humphries, Stan, 70

Lane, Tim, 45
Lay, Mike, 37
lenders, 13–15
Licensed Residential Exam, 38, 40
licenses, 25, 27, 30–31, 36, 37, 50, 51, 70

Marcus, Alec, 65
mortgages, 12–13, 50
Multiple Listing Service (MLS), 20
Musinski, Bob, 18

Sweeney, Maureen, 48

technology, 10–11, 66–70
trainees, 6, 25, 32–37, 38–40, 49

US Bureau of Labor Statistics, 60

Williamson, Jacob, 62–65

IMAGE CREDITS

Cover: © Andrey Popov/iStockphoto
5: © Andrey Popov/Shutterstock Images
7: © Nicolas McComber/iStockphoto
8: © Atstock Productions/Shutterstock Images
11: © Mindful Media/iStockphoto
13: © Jacob Lund/Shutterstock Images
14: © Feverpitched/iStockphoto
16: © Alex Potemkin/iStockphoto
19: © jimfeng/iStockphoto
20: © Arpad Benedek/iStockphoto
24: © damircudic/iStockphoto
29: © SDI Productions/iStockphoto
32: © Singkham/Shutterstock Images
35: © mrmohock/Shutterstock Images
39: © Balance Form Creative/Shutterstock Images
41: © sturti/iStockphoto
43: © SaiArLawKa2/Shutterstock Images
46: © NAN728/Shutterstock Images
49: © SENRYU/iStockphoto
53: © visualspace/iStockphoto
54: © AJ Watt/iStockphoto
57: © Phynart Studio/iStockphoto
59: © Lifestyle Visuals/iStockphoto
63: © Ground Picture/Shutterstock Images
64: © Koh Sze Kiat/iStockphoto
67: © Hispanolistic/iStockphoto
68: © Andrey Popov/iStockphoto
71: © Dmitry-Arhangel 29/Shutterstock Images
73: © Andrey Popov/Shutterstock Images

ABOUT THE AUTHOR

Tammy Gagne has written hundreds of books for both adults and children. Some of her recent books are about paying for college and working as a graphic designer. She lives in northern New England with her husband, son, and dogs.